Designing Global Sales Incentive Plans

Step-By-Step Guide

By
Cedric Ng Mong Shen

Copyright Cedric Ng Mong Shen 2020

Table of Contents

Introduction
Step 1) Diagnose the root cause of poor sales
Step 2) Determine change management strategy
Step 3) Determine eligibility
Step 4) Pay strategy
Step 5) Performance measures
Step 6) Plan mechanics
Step 7) Payout scenarios
Step 8) Plan documentation & communication
Step 9) Plan effectiveness
Other Publications by the Author

Introduction

Your company has hundreds of patchwork sales incentive plans developed by various regions/countries after decades of mergers & acquisitions. As the Global Rewards Director, you are assigned by your CEO to reduce the number of sales incentive plans and align it to corporate strategy. Do you know what to do?

The key to designing an effective global sales-compensation framework is to identify performance measures and design principles that can apply globally and yet provide some flexibility for business unit or local customization. These global design principles serve to protect the organization from bad practice rather than impose a single practice. Examples of global design principles is to have a consistent menu of performance measure for each role, limiting each plan to five measures, specifying that each measure should be weighted at least 15%, or specifying that the total of discretionary measures cannot be weighted more than 35%. In conjunction with the list of globally consistent items, there should be a list of components that can be tailored locally. For example, pay levels can be tied to local market rates, pay-mix can be tailored to the local selling strategy within expected ranges, performance measure weighting can be determined locally within the global guidelines, incentive payout frequency can be based on local selling cycles, and accelerators can be developed based on local expected performance range within global guidelines.

This book teaches you a nine step, 3D6P approach to design effective global sales incentive plans:

Nine step 3D6P approach to design effective global sales incentive plans	
Step 1	**D**iagnose the root cause of poor sales
Step 2	**D**etermine change management strategy
Step 3	**D**etermine eligibility
Step 4	**P**ay strategy
Step 5	**P**erformance measures
Step 6	**P**lan mechanics
Step 7	**P**ayout scenario
Step 8	**P**lan documentation & communication
Step 9	**P**lan effectiveness

Step 1) Diagnose the root cause of poor sales

When the sales team is not delivering, don't assume that your sales incentive design is the problem. As a strategic business partner, Rewards professionals needs to be able to systematically ask intelligent questions to understand business strategy, diagnose the root cause of non-performance, & advise management on the appropriate "medicine" to nurse the organization back to health. Improvement in sales performance can only be achieved when sales incentives is considered in a larger context that includes business strategy, design, process, rewards, people, and culture. Review the root cause of poor sales using the seven dimensions of Organizational effectiveness (i.e. strategy, design, process, rewards, people, culture, and environment).

Dimension 1: Strategy

How management looks at strategy affects sales function effectiveness. Customers can be defined or segmented by Geography, Demographics, Psychographics, or Behavioral. **Sometimes, changing the way a company segments their market is a more effective way to improve performance**. E.g. a company that segments the battery market into "industrial battery market" and "consumer battery market" would probably do better than a company that uses a single strategy for the "whole battery market". When you define Macdonald's customers as "students, male and female, kids, parents, lawyers, shop floor workers", you are segmenting the customers by "Demographics segmentation". You can also define Macdonald's customers using the "Behavioral segmentation" – i.e. what need the customers are trying to fulfill? Looking at McDonald's the need might primarily be to satisfy your hunger. Another reason might be to spend time with friends, get the kids to shut up, escape from the cold, not having to cook, or kill time. Identifying these circumstances can again help in two ways: either bring ideas for new or enhanced offerings or you can target additional customers that have the same need, but have traditionally been neglected because the industry focused on a particular type of customer.

Dimension 2: Design

Design refers to the organizational structure. The design that works during start-up is different from what works during growth, maturity, and decline. Some organizations group start-ups together since start-ups face similar technical and commercial concerns and thus can share learning. Some organizations group start-ups, growth, mature and decline stages together so that start-ups can gain from the more experienced countries. Which route is chosen is a design decision that should be based on explicitly articulated rationale and clear criteria, and it should be revisited when the business life cycle changes and when the political and competitive environment changes.

- **Start-up:**

New start-up usually have limited capital, thus they start small and use either use **selling partners** or hire their own **generalist sales** forces. Start-ups need a lot of effort to create brand awareness before sales can be generated.

- **Growth:**

    At growth stage, it's difficult for generalists sales force to sell the entire product line to multiple products and markets. Thus, Companies need to set up **specialist sales forces** that focus on products, markets, customer segments, or activities such as acquiring customers (hunters) or servicing existing customers (farmers). Every kind of specialization has pro and con. Many companies therefore create hybrid structures that include a mix of generalist as well as market, product, customer and activity specialist. As repeat sales become a larger proportion of sales, customers will require **service** and **support. Account managers** can be used to focus on all the needs of its major customers, while product specialists call on midsize clients that don't generate sufficient business to warrant account managers, and generalist salespeople cover small companies whose small accounts don't justify visits by several product specialist.

- **Maturity:**

When businesses hit maturity, the emphasis shift to making sales forces more effective by appointing account managers, for the largest accounts and improving cost-efficiency by using less expensive **telesales staff** and **sales assistants**. Account managers coordinate the sales effort and bring in product specialists when deep expertise is needed. Sales assistants and **part-time salespeople** are deployed to woo small or geographically dispersed customers and to sell easy-to-understand products. Telesales staff is used to perform activities that don't need face-to-face contact with customers.

- **Decline:**

  When turnaround is unlikely and decline is inevitable, organizations **reduce the size of sales forces** and use even more cost-efficient ways to cover markets. Businesses at the decline stage use their salespeople to service the most profitable and strategically important customers. By using less-expensive selling resources, companies can continue selling to some segments. That entails moving the coverage of some customers from specialty salespeople to **generalist**, and shifting the coverage of other customers from field salespeople to **telesales staff**, shifting the selling of easy-to-understand products and administrative tasks to **sales assistants, telesales staff, part-time salespeople, and the internet**.

Dimension 3: Process

Work processes affect sales function effectiveness, inter-departmental coordination, and sales staff learning curve. The more similar work processes are across a company's units, the easier a sales employee can assimilate into a new position in a different business unit and focus on learning what is different. Inadequate information systems prevent an organization from moving from a country-based structure to a product-based structure if the systems are unable to report performance by product. Review your processes by asking: why do you do what you do? Why must customers be served? Can customers help themselves? Why do you assume that staff cannot make good decisions? Why do we do it the way we did it?

- **Dimension 4: Rewards**

    The purpose of the reward system is to align the goals of the sales people with the goals of the organization. The reward system must be congruent with the Sales structure and processes. Companies at the start-up/growth stage might include performance measures such as growth of existing customer base, new customer acquisition, new territory expansion, & pipeline. Companies at the mature/decline stage usually focus on performance measures such as margin or revenue.

Dimension 5: People

Sales function effectiveness is influenced by the people that a company has. Talent management begins with identifying the type of people the firm needs, hiring them, orientating them, developing them, and retaining them.

- Do you have the career paths & development initiatives to attract and retain your talent? The quality of your sales training program affects your sales people's ability to close sales. An effective sales training programs covers product knowledge, competitor knowledge, and market industry knowledge, and how to deliver a persuasive sales presentation. The worst scenario is a sales person not knowing what their products or services are about. Do your sales people know all the key features & benefits of the products? Do they know how efficient or safe their products are? Do they know where the ingredients come from? If you don't know who you are fighting against, chances are you will be beaten up. Does your sales team know who their competitors are? What are their strengths & weakness? Why their product features is not superior to yours? Does your sales team know what the latest trends are that may affect your market or industry? Minimally, do a monthly training on new product updates, competitor findings & market & industry information. Make this a formal session. You can also discuss this knowledge during weekly sales meetings. Ask your sales people what new things they gathered this week? Add that to your training materials.

- How does your Leader's vision compare with your competitors? If a leader is promoted from within, he is likely to maintain the current business direction. If a leader is hired from other companies in the same industry, he is likely to make some changes to your business direction. If a leader is hired from other industry, you are likely to have radical change.

- How does your sale's people capability compare with your competitor's people one-for-one for similar roles? Are the right people in the right positions? Will re-assigning work from an overloaded salesperson to an under-worked salesperson improve your overall sales performance? If there is intense pressure for rapid growth, the company may need more sales people rather than a more aggressive incentive plan.

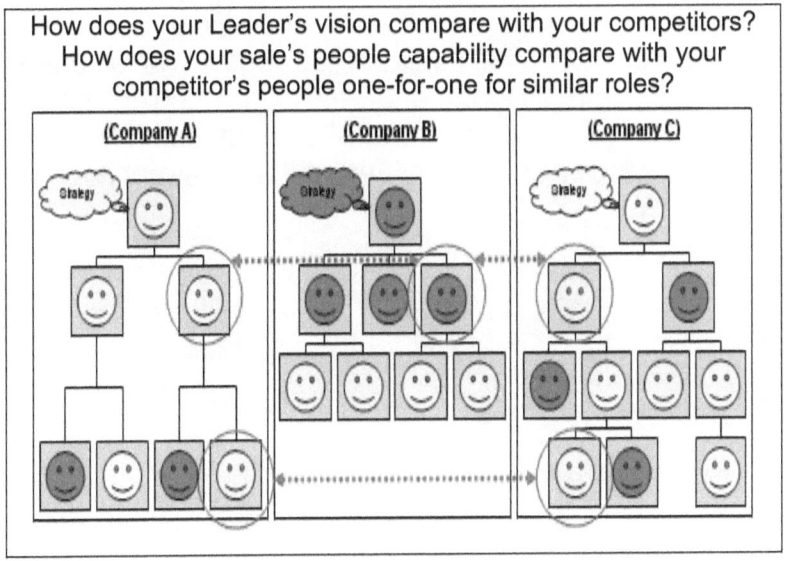

Dimension 6: Culture

Culture can be consciously designed or modified to drive performance. Culture influences how work gets done, affects project success or failure, says who fits in and who doesn't, and determines the company's overall mood. Cultural issues may be responsible for low morale, absenteeism or high staff turnover. An organization may realize that their current sales culture constitutes a barrier against performance. Decide which parts of your sales culture you want to encourage, and which parts you want to change by asking questions such as: What cultural strengths have been highlighted by your analysis of the current sales culture? What cultural characteristics are hindering your strategy and ability to attract talent?

Dimension 7: Environment

Your Sales Incentive plan design also need to consider external environment factors such as government regulations and technological changes. Some countries regulations may require sales commissions to be paid monthly. If your company plans to move from country structure to Product structure, is your company's information systems able to report performance by product?

Step 2) Determine change management strategy

Once you have diagnosed that an ineffective sales incentive plan is the root cause of poor sales, the next step is to determine the appropriate change management strategy to implement your new sales incentive plan. Frequently projects fail because of poor change management skills rather than technical compensation and benefits knowledge. Compensation and benefits professionals need to be equipped with change management skills to successfully implement any new global sales incentive plan. Kurt Lewin's Force Field Analysis is a useful technique for looking at all the forces for and against a decision. In effect, it is a specialized method of weighing pros and cons.

To carry out a force field analysis, follow these steps:

- List all forces-for- change.
- List all forces-against-change.
- Describe your action-plan.

Force field analysis action plan

1) **Goal:** *Implement the global Sales incentive design by year xx*

2) **Forces-for-change:**
   - *CEO says so.*
   -
   -

3) **Forces-against-change:**
   - *Lack the technical knowledge to design sales incentives.*
   -
   -

4) **Action plan:**
   - *Attend the training on how to design sales incentives.*
   - *Current team is ineffective and has just run out of steam because the schedule is too long or hasn't realized any quick hits. Getting new blood on the team is all that is needed to rejuvenate the effort.*
   -

Step 3) Determine eligibility

HR, Sales, & Finance are typically involved in the sales incentive design process.

- **The role of Sales head** - is to provide inputs on the business strategy/priorities & business lifecycle stage, identify who is eligible for B2B sales incentive, and set the sales, pipeline & strategic targets for the sales team. Other than driving performance, the sales incentive plan should be fiscally responsible, externally competitive, and internally equitable with non-sales jobs. Thus, salespeople who are beneficiaries of the sales incentives should provide input rather than controlling the overall sales incentive design process.

- **The role of Finance** - is to provide & validate the sales achievement figures for the computation of sales incentive payout.

- **The role of HR** - is to review the overall Sales incentive design, act as an impartial party for the sales incentive design, recommend the pay-mix strategy, recommend the pay curve, recommend the pay frequency, ensure that salespeople's remuneration package is externally competitive and internally equitable with non-sales jobs, and do sales incentive payouts cost modeling.

To determine who is eligible for the sales incentive, it is important to consider the impact that each sales role have on influencing sales. **Each distinct sales role in a company requires its own type of sales incentive plan. A key step to develop global sales incentives is to map the hundreds of sales jobs (with widely varying job titles & responsibilities) into a handful of globally standardized benchmark sales roles**. Having aligned global roles definitions enable clearer career progressions, and make it easier to implement global compensation programs. After mapping the local jobs to globally standardized benchmark sales roles, determine who to include in the plan by considering CRI factors (Customer, Revenue, and Influence):

- Customer facing;

- Revenue target responsibility; and

- Influence in the purchase decision.

Step 4) Pay strategy

A company's pay positioning is its pay strategy. Establish your pay positioning (e.g. 40th, 50th, or 75th percentile of the market) by considering CCESSS factors (Competitor practices, Cost consciousness, Expected staff performance, Stage of business, Strategic position, and Supply of talent).

CCESSS factors affecting pay positioning	Competitor practices	Low	Average	High
	Cost consciousness	High	Average	Low
	Expected staff performance	Low	Average	High
	Stage of business	Start up/ Decline	Growth/ Mature	Mature
	Strategic position	Low	Average	High
	Supply of talent	Abundant	Adequate	Scarce
		40th percentile	50th percentile	75th percentile
		Pay positioning		

Are there unique industry characteristics that require salespeople with special scientific or technical skills? Some companies pay Sales representatives of medical specialty products at 75th percentile. In a commodity business, where there is little product differentiation, a salesperson's personality may be the only reason for the customer to buy, and thus may require a more aggressive compensation plan at 75th percentile. In consumer packaged goods business, where companies do intense advertising, individual salespeople may not have as much impact, and thus they might be paid at 40th percentile.

Target total-cash compensation is the amount of base pay plus target incentive payments for employees who achieve on-target performance. There are two approaches to benchmark the compensation for salespeople.

- **Derive total-cash from annual-base-salary:-** One approach is to benchmark to market annual-base-salary then use your target pay-mix to calculate the target-total-cash for each sales role. Using this approach, if the market annual-base-salary of an Accounts Manager is $60,000, and your target pay-mix is 60:40, then target-total-cash is $100,000 ($60,000/0.6).

- **Derive annual-base-salary from total-cash:-** The other approach is to benchmark to market total-cash, and then use your target pay-mix to set the target-annual-base-salary within a tolerable range for each sales role. Thus, if the market total-cash of an Accounts Manager is $100,000, and your target pay-mix is 60:40, then target-annual-base-salary is $60,000 ($100,000 x 0.6).

Total-cash and annual-base-salary are two important factors to consider for compensation benchmarking. However, when total-cash and annual-base-salary are in conflict, companies need to decide which is more important.

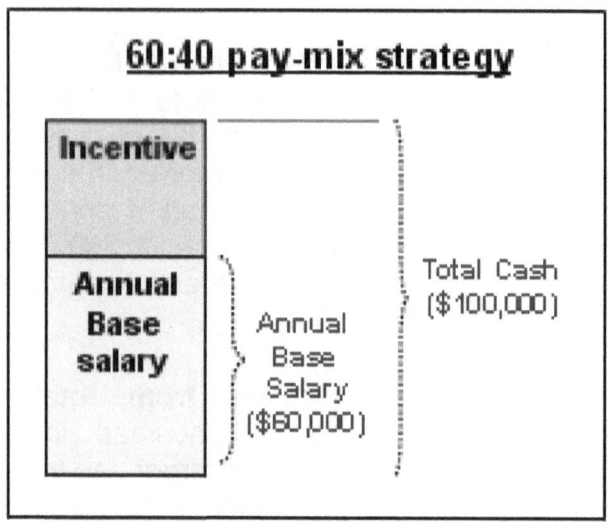

Step 5) Performance measures

Sales incentive plan for B2C businesses is not effective to drive performance for B2B businesses and companies in different maturity stages need different incentive plans. Some companies emphasize customer service in addition to its quantitative sales goals to differentiate itself from its competitors. Start the design process by interviewing the business heads to understand the business strategy, how the company segments the market, which market segments or product lines are not doing well, what is the product life cycle stage, how long is the selling cycle, and what are the strategic qualitative objectives?

It is critical to tailor specific performance measures to the company's strategy and financial goals to maximize plan effectiveness. Compensation plans work best when they are simple. More than three measures can be confusing and may reduce the emphasis of key measures, and may even indicate the need to create another sales role. Most sales incentive plans have some form of sales revenue measure, with a profit measure included only if the sales person has some control over pricing. Companies at the start-up/growth stage might include performance measures such as growth of existing customer base, new customer acquisition, or new territory expansion. In contrast, companies at the mature/decline stage usually focus on performance measures such as margin or revenue. The finance team must be able to provide reports for each salesperson's performance measures.

In addition, different weights should be assigned to different measures depending on their relative importance to the overall business goals. If three measures are used, the weighting does not have to be 1/3rd for each measure. A more critical measure could have a weighting of 60%, with 20% allocated to each of the remaining two measures. B2B business that have longer selling cycle than B2C business should assign higher weight for pipeline quotas and strategic quota, while setting lower weight for sales quotas.

To build effective incentive plans, sales incentive designers cannot overlook the sales quota-setting process. Poorly set sales quotas can create either overpayment "windfalls" for salespeople or unrealistically high expectations that de-motivate salespeople. Payouts in a quota-based plan are related directly to the percent of quota achieved in a given performance period. If you want your sales team members to achieve or exceed their assigned quotas, you need to ensure that the process for setting those quotas is effective. Start the quota-setting process by looking at historical sales trends. What was the total revenue from all the sales territories in the previous year? How much did your competitors sell? After looking at the historical sales, add a growth expectation on what is doable for your products in the current market. Some industries can realistically expect sales growth of 10% while others may see 100%. The quotas should be challenging & yet achievable. People in the same grade & same job role should be assigned similar sales quota. People at a higher grade should be given higher or more difficult sales quotas than people at a lower grade. After adding the historical sales figures with a growth expectation, you might be tempted to divide this total revenue by the number of salespeople to define the quota for each person. But, not all sales roles are equal, and not all sales territories are equal. In some territories, the competition may be strong and hence reduce the potential for sales. In other territories, competition may be weak or non-existent.

Two methods are commonly used to assign sales territories.

- Equal workload method equalizes the workload of all salesmen in the same grade/role. Territories are formulated so that they are equal in workload rather than in potential.

- Equal potential method starts on the basis that salesperson productivity varies depending on the territory potential.

Assigning Sales head targets to individual Sales representatives.				
Company name	Sales head	Sales Rep 1	Sales Rep 2	Sales Rep 3
Company 1	$1,359,200		$1,359,200	
Company 2	$1,286,400	$1,286,400		
Company 3	$1,135,888			$1,135,888
Company 4	$936,000			$936,000
Company 5	$757,272	$757,272		
Company 6	$730,000		$730,000	
Total	$6,204,760	$2,043,672	$2,089,200	$2,071,888

Step 6) Plan mechanics

Plan mechanics include hurdles/gates, thresholds, target, leverage/upside, maximums, pay-mix, payout timing.

Maximum or cap on incentive pay is used by companies to preclude excessive earnings for unexpected large orders not obtained through the sales rep's efforts, and to overcome erroneous quota setting. Generally, sales incentive plans should be designed without a cap so as to encourage those who can be extraordinary to be extraordinary. **Hurdles/Gates** are pre-conditions that must be met before any incentives will be paid and represent the minimum acceptable level of overall corporate performance that is of prime importance to management. Hurdles can be used to cover the fixed salary cost and can be determined based on break-even volume. A related design principle, called performance **thresholds** are used to set minimal levels of performance that must be achieved by the individual before an incentive is paid and can weed out underachievers. Thresholds can either be set at a level where there is a 70 to 80% probability of achieving the result, or set at a level that is equal to the actual average performance of the salespeople last year, or set at the sales forecast level that is considered recurring revenue. **Target** is set at the budget performance levels of the incentive year. Target should be seen as a realistic stretch measure and set at a level where there is a 50% probability of achieving the result. **Leverage/upside** is the maximum amount of reward for beyond target performance (excellence performance) or the portion of compensation above target pay. Performance level for upside, can either be set at a level where there is a 10-20% probability of achieving the result, or at 10% higher than the target performance. Upside earning can either be set at 1-3 times the target opportunity, or set at the 75th or 90th percentile.

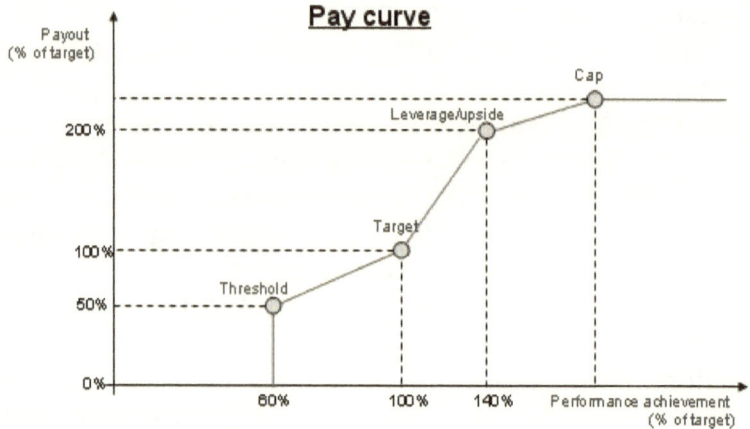

After establishing plan measures, companies need to set the sales incentive formula. Sales commission is a type of incentive, expressed as a percentage of sales dollars, a percentage of gross margin, or a dollar amount per unit sold. A typical sales commission formula is constructed as follows: target incentive / target performance = commission rate. For example, if the target incentive is $50,000 and the target performance is $1,000,000, then the "commission rate" would be 0.05%. Sales incentive/bonus is different from Sales commission. Sales incentive/bonus is a type of incentive tied to actual performance compared to a goal (e.g. sales quota) & expressed as a percentage of salary.

A typical sales incentive formula is constructed as follows: Annual base salary x incentive rate x target performance = target incentive.

Here's how to set the sales incentive formula at threshold, target, and leverage/upside:

i) Threshold incentive rate: if a sales representative annual base salary is $100,000, threshold incentive is $25,000 and threshold performance is $600,000, then the "threshold incentive rate" would be 0.0000004% [$25,000 threshold incentive / ($100,000 annual base salary x $600,000 threshold performance)].

ii) Target incentive rate: if a sales representative annual base salary is $100,000, target incentive is $50,000 and target performance is $1,000,000, then the "target incentive rate" would be 0.0000005% [$50,000 target incentive / ($100,000 annual base salary x $1,000,000 target performance)].

iii) Leverage incentive rate: if a sales representative annual base salary is $100,000, leverage incentive is $100,000 and the excellence performance is $1,400,000, then the "leverage incentive rate" would be 0.0000007% [$100,000 leverage incentive / ($100,000 annual base salary x $1,400,000 excellence performance)].

Pay-mix is another component of plan mechanics. Pay-mix is the relationship of base-salary and target-incentive (commission or bonus). It is expressed as a percentage of target cash compensation. A 25:75 pay mix means that target cash compensation is composed of 25% base salary and 75% incentive.

Sales Role	Employee's influence on customer's buying decision.	Pay mix
Key Account Manager	Highly directional	64% : 36%
Territory Sales Engineer	Highly directional	67% : 33%
Channel Sales Engineer	Highly directional	67% : 33%
Product Sales Engineer	Highly directional	67% : 33%
Pre-Sales Technical support	Performance reminder	82%: 18%
Post-Sales Customer Service Engineer	Performance reminder	86% : 14%

Generally, commission-only plans are more appropriate for sellers that work as independent agents and have ownership of their own accounts. It is important that setting the pay-mix comes after sales job design because the level of influence on customer's buying decision in each sales role is directly linked to its mix of incentive pay and base salary. **Pay-mix should be unique to a company, rather than a number taken directly from a market survey report. Pay-mix strategy is an important design component that drives the organization's strategy because pay-mix decision is derived from risk sales levels, business growth stage, sales role's influence on customer buying decision, sales strategy executed by the sales role, and barriers to entry to the sales job**. Lower incentive component should be considered (e.g. 10% - 25% of salary) for widely advertised products where reorders are automatic, for mature companies trying to maintain market share and customer relationships, for roles whereby specific skills are needed, and for roles with limited influence on customer's buying decision (e.g. pre-sales technical jobs). Higher incentive component should be considered (e.g. 25% - 50% of salary) for products facing intense competition, for roles where little post-sales service is required, for roles that rely heavily on influencing skills to produce a sales (e.g. direct sales reps, sales roles that focus on pursuing new accounts), and for startups that want to grow aggressively. Companies should also evaluate whether customers buy because of product advertising or because of the effort of the salesperson? More commission or incentive is used where sales are highly impacted by individual sales efforts, such as insurance. Pay-mix should be fixed for a role if there are no changes in business strategy and sales role, and it should never be used as a variable component that is adjusted every year just to match the incumbents to the market total-cash. The adverse effect of altering pay-mix particularly from a low salary/high incentive to a higher salary/lower incentive, is to reduce the motivation for sales people to perform at high levels! The right approach to address incumbents who are below market for total-cash, is to gradually increase the incumbent's base salary via market adjustment. It is fine, for people doing the same role to have different levels of total-cash, because different employees have different experience/capabilities/value-add although they might be doing similar role. If a person is below market for base salary by 40%, you don't immediately increase his base salary by 40% to reach market median. You would most probably increase his base salary to market median gradually over the years. Same principle should apply to target-total-cash.

Payout timing is another component of plan mechanics. How frequently do we pay out rewards? In general, the closer to the sales event the better, and payout for sales incentive plans is typically monthly or quarterly. Factors to consider for payout timing are duration of the sales cycles, size of sales transactions, number of transactions, pay-mix, and administrative capabilities.

Role	Pay mix	Sales cycle	Size of sales transactions	Number of transactions	Administrative capability	Payment frequency
Role 1	95:5	6 months	$10,000	1000	Able to manage 6 month payout.	6 months
Role 2	90:10	3 months	$300,000	3,000	Able to manage 3 month payout.	3 months
Role 3	75:25	3 months	$300,000	3,000	Able to manage 3 month payout.	3 months
Role 4	60:40	1 month	$1,000,000	10,000	Able to manage 1 month payout.	1 month
Role 5	0:100	Less than 1 month	$1,000,000	10,000	Able to manage 1 month payout.	1 month

Step 7) Payout scenarios

In real-world conditions, the plan can produce unexpected financial results. Thus, there needs to be a rigorous modeling of various performance scenarios. Incentive payout cost simulation can be done at threshold performance, on-target performance, and excellence performance. Plan modeling enables companies to assess the impact of each scenario at both the macro level (in terms of company cost) and the micro level (in terms of potential individual earnings).

Sales Role	Target average incentive earnings			
	Year 2010	Year 2011		
	Target	Threshold	Target	Excellence
Director of Sales	$5,000	$4,200	$6,000	$7,800
Sales Rep	$2,000	$1,055	$2,650	$$3,445
Sales Engineer	$1,000	$770	$1,100	$1,430

Step 8) Plan documentation & communication

All incentive plans need a plan document that outlines the purpose of the plan, how it works and what actions will be taken to address unforeseen circumstances. Good plan documents should include plan objectives, plan period, eligibility, goal setting, incentive award formula, timing of payouts, recovery of commission, resignation & termination, territory transfers or splits, special provisions, and plan administration. Many plans fail because of poor communication rather than poor plan design. Management must take the time to meet with the sales force to explain the sales compensation plan. If we ourselves do not understand how & why the plan works, how can we expect it to work?

Step 9) Plan effectiveness

To assess existing plans, compare actual sales compensation to actual business performance to ensure there is a positive correlation. Performance distributions can be used to evaluate how performance relative to quota is distributed to determine if there are issues with quota setting. The ideal is to get a normal distribution. Typically, two-thirds of your sales reps should achieve quota, with a fraction exceeding quota. If 90% of your sales rep achieve quota, and 60% exceed quota, you may find that sales achievement expectations are too low. You can interview key sales reps for their opinions on issues such as their interaction with sales operations team, etc. Feedback from these interviews will give you important inputs on your new design.

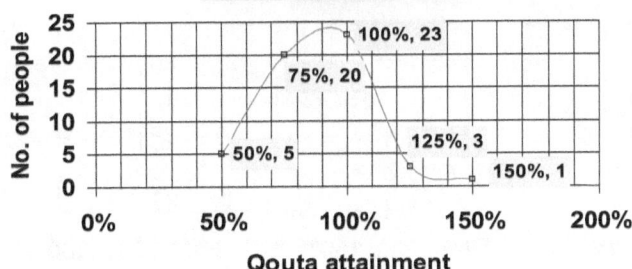

- ❖ Quotas may be too high so individuals may not be earning competitive pay levels.

- ❖ Need to reassess if business plans are realistic and reexamine quota allocation process.

Performance distributions (Bi-Modal)

Chart showing No. of people vs. Qouta attainment with data points: 50%, 5; 75%, 15; 100%, 5; 125%, 20; 150%, 5.

- ❖ Common in new organizations where quota setting is still being defined.

Other Publications by the Author

https://www.amazon.com/Organization-Design-Performance-Step-Step-ebook/dp/B07GFSN93Y/ref=sr_1_4_twi_kin_1?s=books&ie=UTF8&qid=1543771861&sr=1-4&keywords=cedric+ng+mong+shen

Organizations must be able to adapt their structures to capture new markets and expand existing ones. The design that works during start-up is different from what works during growth, maturity, and decline. However, when Companies are not structured properly, business opportunities fizzle due to lack of attention, and turf wars stifle teamwork because of unclear responsibilities. Often Performance issues are a Structural issue rather than a Person issue. A company can have great people, great leadership and still not perform well because of poor organizational design. Organization design is more than moving the boxes. It is about how to configure your Department or Company structure to improve performance, and can be applied by Department managers at all levels. Organization Design work sometimes encompasses redesign of an entire company, but mostly the focus is at departmental level. This book highlights the warning signs when organization design is needed, and provides a simple four-step framework to guide managers how to design effective Departments and Organizations:
- Step 1 – Define Criteria
- Step 2 – Diagnose Issues
- Step 3 – Design Structure
- Step 4 – Deliver Structure

https://www.amazon.com/Designing-Salary-Structures-Step-Step-ebook/dp/B07G264J11/ref=sr_1_3?keywords=cedric+ng+mong+shen&qid=1553280240&s=books&sr=1-3

Your CEO returned from a management retreat with a new strategic business plan that will revitalize the company and lead it into lucrative new markets. As the Director of Compensation and Benefits, you are charged with translating the strategic business plan into a pay strategy that supports the company's vision and business strategy. Do you know what to do?

To design the Salary structures that drive business results and performance, you need to know which positions are "hot skills", which positions are difficult-to-hire, which positions have high attrition rate, and which functions are strategic functions. Each of these has implications for designing a salary structure that drives business results and performance. Salary structures provide guidelines for making pay related decisions within an organization, bridging the gap between where you are today and where you want to be tomorrow (target pay positioning). This book shows you in six simplified steps, how to design strategic salary structures:

1) Establish your pay positioning.
2) Establish job worth hierarchy.
3) Develop job grades.
4) Develop pay range.
5) Calculate structural parameters (pay range, min, max).
6) "Slot" your employees and tweak your salary structure

https://www.amazon.com/Reviewing-Employee-Benefits-using-model-ebook/dp/B07FXSYKB2/ref=sr_1_3?keywords=cedric+ng+mong+shen&qid=1553017293&s=books&sr=1-3

Your CEO returned from a management retreat with a new strategic business plan that will revitalize the company and lead it into lucrative new markets. As the Global Rewards Director, you are tasked with designing a "Global Benefits Philosophy & Strategy" that can be applied across different business units and countries. --- Do you know what to do?

Do you have difficulty getting Union buy-in to reduce employee benefits? Do you have difficulty convincing your CEO to enhance employee benefits? Do you have difficulty explaining why company can't give employees cash allowances instead of benefits?

This book addresses all these issues and provides a framework to help you to formulate your company's global employee benefits positioning and strategy. Employee Benefits reflect the culture of the organization and differentiate its Employer brand. A company without differentiated Benefits Strategy is like a ship that follows where the wind blows without any direction of its own.

https://www.amazon.com/Predictive-HR-Analytics-Mong-Shen-ebook/dp/B07KWZ86DK/ref=sr_1_1?keywords=cedric+ng+mong+shen&qid=1553279368&s=books&sr=1-1

Most people struggle with analytics because they don't have a structured framework to an unstructured problem. Predictive analytics helps you see what is invisible to others, so you know which behaviors differentiate your most successful employees, creating a competitive advantage over those that rely on gut feel. This book explains how to use the structured five-step ARHAT approach for Predictive HR Analytics (Ask Questions, Review Literature, Hypothesis Formulation, Analyze Data, Tell the Story). Numerous real-world examples are included, which will be useful in your hypothesis formulation (i.e. If X and Y is done, then Z will happen). Most books just discuss about HR analytics without showing you how to run statistical analysis. This book not only discuss about HR analytics, but teaches you data-storytelling and data-visualization techniques, and statistical techniques such as Decision trees, Correlation, Multiple Regression, Chi-Square, and R programming. It covers the entire scope of Predictive HR Analytics (Benefits, Compensation, Culture, Diversity & Inclusion, Engagement, Leadership, Learning and Development, Personality Traits, Recruitment, Sales Incentives), and shows you how Predictive HR Analytics can be used to answer questions such as:

(1) Predict who are the people at risk of leaving.
(2) Identify where the best people come from and how successful a candidate will be if hired.
(3) Predict impact of employee engagement on customer satisfaction, revenue and Shareholder Returns.
(4) Predict financial impact of training.
(5) Predict Diversity & Inclusion's impact on revenue.
(6) Predict employee absenteeism and accident.

https://www.amazon.com/dp/B07PXRLL3Z/ref=sr_1_5?keywords=cedric+ng+mong+shen&qid=1553272657&s=books&sr=1-5

You don't need to buy expensive statistical software like SPSS. This book teaches you R (R can be downloaded for free), People Analytics, Social Media Analytics, Text Mining and Sentiment Analysis. It is written for people with no knowledge of R, with step-by-step print-screen instructions. You don't need Statistical knowledge, as R executes the statistical number crunching (Correlation, Multiple & Logistic Regression, etc.) for you, by simply entering a few commands. This book covers the full People Analytics scope (Benefits, Compensation, Culture, Diversity & Inclusion, Engagement, Leadership, Learning & Development, Personality Traits, Performance Management, Recruitment, Sales Incentives) with numerous real-world examples, and shows how **R** can help you:
1) Run Social Media Analytics, Text mining & Sentiment Analysis with R.
2) Predict employees' flight-risk using R's Correlation & Logistic Regression function.
3) Identify the personality traits of top performing Customer Service staff and Sales staff using R's correlation function.
4) Predict impact of Employee Engagement on Customer Satisfaction, Revenue and Shareholder Returns, etc. using R's Correlation & Multiple Regression function.
5) Predict impact of Learning & Development on Sales, using R's Multiple Regression function.
6) Predict Diversity & Inclusion's impact on Revenue and EBIT using R's Multiple Regression function.

https://www.amazon.com/dp/B07TW7V7F5/ref=sr_1_2?keywords=ng+mong+shen&qid=1562036969&s=books&sr=1-2

A lot of organizational data is often untapped unstructured data in the form of text & numbers. For those who don't want to spend months learning R programming & for those who can't afford to buy expensive SPSS statistical software. This is the only book that teaches you how to use Microsoft Excel for Predictive HR Analytics, Text Mining & Organizational Network Analysis (ONA) with step-by-step print-screen instructions:

1) **Predictive HR Analytics:** Use Excel's Statistical Analysis tools (Decision trees, Correlation, Multiple & Logistic Regression) to run Predictive HR Analytics. E.g. an employee is predicted to have a 60% probability of getting into accidents, if he is age 25, worked 1 year in the company & took 6 days sick leave. An employee is predicted to get rated "7" for Customer Service, if the training program that he attended has a training evaluation score of "8". An employee is predicted to resign if she is age 23, worked for 2 years, and takes 60 minutes to commute to work.

2) **Organizational Network Analysis (ONA):** Run ONA using Excel's network analysis tool. Learn how to convert an employee's organizational network into a score & then predict if they will be a high-potential (HiPo). E.g. an employee is predicted to be a HiPo with performance rating of "9", if his "Social Network Size" is "16", "Social Network Diversity Index" is "3" & "Competency Score" is "8".

3) **Text Mining, Sentiment Analysis & Word Clouds:** Mine text from social network posts, employee engagement surveys & Glassdoor comments, then run Sentiment Analysis using Excel & visualize the insights with "Word Clouds". Learn how to predict a company's average employee attrition rate based on its sentiment. E.g. a company's average employee attrition rate is predicted to be 8%, if unemployment rate is 3%, GDP growth is 2%, Glassdoor public sentiment rating is "5", and engagement score is "7".

https://www.amazon.com/dp/B0859CB567/ref=sr_1_2?keywords=ng+mong+shen&qid=1582910007&s=books&sr=1-2

The 21st century is redefined by a data-driven revolution & gig economy. But, to date, employee engagement has not been based on a data-driven model. This makes it difficult to justify investment in employee engagement programs with the rigor that a data-driven CEO expects. IISS is the 1st & only book that incorporates Employee Experience & Engagement with Predictive Analytics. It offers a fresh way to cultivate engagement using "4 Engagement Bags" & "5 Engagement Fertilizers".

Bag 1) Inspire with Engagement Investment: Inspire with Predictive Analytics, and Inspire with Stories & Data Visualisation Techniques

Bag 2) Inspire with Engagement Fertilizers: Making employees happy, doesn't mean they will work hard for the organization. Use the 5 "Engagement Fertilizers" to build great employee experience & engagement:
- **Fertilizer 1: Basic Needs** – Soil, Rain, Sun
- **Fertilizer 2: Social Needs** – Birds
- **Fertilizer 3: Growth Needs** – Nutrients
- **Fertilizer 4: Meaning** – Healthy Tree
- **Fertilizer 5: Expectations** – Fruits!

Bag 3) Sentiment Gathering: Pulse Surveys, Focus Groups, Glassdoor Reviews, IISS Engagement Diagnosis Questions.

Bag 4) Sentiment Diagnosis & Prescription: Engagement Metrics & Dashboards, Bar Charts, Radar Charts, Word Clouds, Sentiment Analysis, Correlation, Regression, IISS Engagement Prescriptions.

www.ingramcontent.com/pod-product-compliance
Lightning Source LLC
Chambersburg PA
CBHW030537220526
45463CB00007B/2874